learning from

eagle,

living with

coyote

TSIMMU

Orion Books / New York

Copyright © 1991, 1993 by Teresa Martino

Published by Orion Books, a division of Crown Publishers, Inc., 201 East 50th Street, New York, New York 10022.
Member of the Crown Publishing Group.
Originally published in 1991 by Grandfather Publishing.
Random House, Inc. New York, Toronto, London, Sydney, Auckland

Orion and colophon are trademarks of Crown Publishers, Inc.

Manufactured in the United States of America

Library of Congress Cataloging-in-Publication Data

Tsimmu.
    Learning from eagle, living with coyote / Tsimmu. — 1st ed.
        p.   cm. — (Library of the American West)
    1. Indians of North America—Legends. I. Title. II. Series.
E98.F6T75 1993
398.2'08997—dc20   93-16653 CIP

Book design by Linda Kocur

Library of the American West editor: Herman J. Viola

ISBN 0-517-59542-7

10 9 8 7 6 5 4 3 2 1

First Orion Books Edition

for my family
and my friends who
are also my family.

to the nameless one
and all my Teachers
with hope and love.

Grandfather, Grandmother

*Beware of assumptions as you read these
reflections, conversations and narratives. All is
not as you might expect. If Wolf or Coyote
vomits, this is an act intended to share
something valuable, the gift of food. When
Rabbit seems to make no sense, it may be
because he says everything backward.
Grandfather and Mother are sometimes the
same person, but not always. Sometimes they
are not human. As Tsimmu told me, while we
made this book, lots of amazing things are
happening behind us, but we don't turn around
fast enough to see. So you may, as I have,
sometimes feel there is someone watching you as
you read, teasing.*

RAYNA

I don't know . . .
I think the tree reaches up
and pulls the sky down—
I can see that from my window.
"Grandfather?
Is that you pulling down the sky?"

pulling

down

the

sky

Fox Boy walked by my house yesterday
from the edge of the meadow,
from the circle of trees.
I think Fox knows something.
He winked . . .
He winked and then stuck his tongue out at me.
But maybe he was licking his whiskers.
"Grandfather,
Grandfather . . .
Ask that fox to tell me his secret.
His secret from the circle of trees."
Grandfather smiles and squints.
"Oh my Granddaughter,
you already know that one. . . !"

"Is it in my pockets,
my pockets Grandfather?
In my mackinaw?
In my jeans?"
Eagle Man saw me looking in my pockets,
in my Jeans.
He screamed . . .
Eagle Man.
"No, no Granddaughter,
not in pockets.

Not that way,
the other way.
In your hands,
in your eyes,
from your spirit.
There's the secret,
right where Coyote left it."
Grandfather walked,
walked up the tree,
looked down, and let go of the sky.

I met my brother
on the grass . . .
in the sun.
He was great, tall, maned.
His eyes glittered.
I heard him breathing,
a sound like the sea, wave upon sand . . .
We met before,
I felt your last breath on my hands,
on a day long ago, a day like this one,
surrounded by my people.
On that day you were free
and I chased you!
And now . . .
see how the day stands on her head
and looks upside down.
You come to me.
When we met before,
you gave me life.
Now I walk before you, like Coyote,
and you follow me.
My life is always before you.

"What do you see when you close your eyes?"
says my Grandfather.
"A bull buffalo eating grain from my hand."

I dreamed one night.
I dreamed I stood on a wide meadow
full of grass, blue flowers,
rocks, insects.
Birds flew, the air moved,
the sky turned.

"What was that?"
Tortoise Old Man looked out.
"Nothing, daughter."
"No, I felt it. I saw it."
Tortoise smiled slow.
"Oh that.
That was your mother breathing."

I see circles,
circles on the water,
circles in the trees,
circles in the world.
If I follow these circle paths,
what do I find?
I wrote this and Coyote came by.
I put it on the ground.
Coyote smiled and walked over to it,
"Say, what's this?"
"Oh, it's talk about circles."
"Circles, eh."
"Yeah, what do I find with circles?"
"That's an easy one," smiled Coyote.
He walked around the paper
and then looked at me and ran away.
I looked.
Hey! A set of coyote tracks around my paper.
In a circle.

I am not a poet.
No words own me.
I never saw fox think about his yap
or wolf about his howling.
So I won't either.
I'll play around the words.
Let them fall.
You see, if you don't care, I don't care.
Coyote came by the other day and read this.
Read it, then vomited on my page.

I went to my mother's house.
She said, "What's that tail?
You've got a wolf's tail there."
I felt back there and there was one.
I went to my brother's house and he said,
"Your arms! They look like hawk wings!
Feathers are falling!"
I looked. So it was.
I went to my friends' house.
They said, "What! An antelope has left
her horns on your head."
I felt there and there were horns.
"That's strange," they said.

I went to Coyote's house.
He said, "Sister, you look great today.
The weather agrees with you."
I looked outside Coyote's hole
It was . . .
        snowing
        raining
        foggy
        sunny
        windy.
So I stayed.

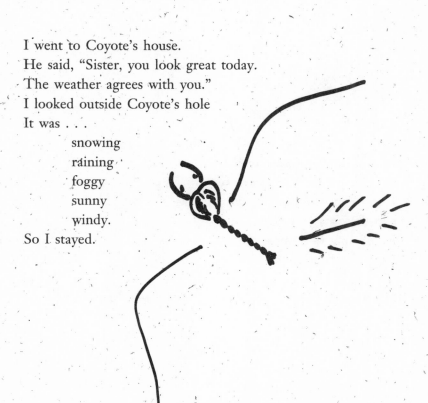

I dreamed . . .
I stood on a mountain
on the very top of a rocky spot,
very high,
very cold.
Clouds below.
Above, gold eagles circled.
I watched them.
They said, "Come."
I lifted my arms, thinking.
But my arms,
they changed without telling me.
I had wings.
So what did I do?
I leaped, I flew.
I remember pushing off rock with taloned feet.
I joined them.
I circled . . .
I looked down and the mountain was gone.
I landed sometime later in a meadow.
Coyote was eating a deer's afterbirth close by.
He saw me and came over.
Looked me up . . . looked me down . . .
I told him about the mountain
and the circles of eagles.
I looked at him out of a brown eagle's eye.
Coyote sat down and scratched himself.
My talons were gone suddenly.
"Funny," he said, "It happens to me all the time."

There are people.
Quiet people.
Silent,
patient people.
Waiting.
They stand outside my cabin.
They hold their hands up,
they hold their arms up,
they are reaching.
They are dancing medicine,
or the medicine is dancing them.
I was outside one day
reading a man's words.
Coyote came by where I lay the book down.
He snatched it up and looked at me with yellow eyes.
(There are no eyes like Coyote's.)
He shredded it, slowly.
"Tasty," he said.
I scolded him, "I was reading that."
Coyote looked at me sidelong.
"So read these people standing around you.
The silent, green ones."

The dark looks back at me sometimes.
The inbetween looks back between the trees of the forest.

It isn't empty,
Isn't.
Space, space
dark, dark.

Void is so empty it's full
and you know, I can hear it.
Hear,
hear it breathing.

I was stars once, and dust.
I was mountain and ocean.
I was the fluff of the dandelion,
tail of the deer,
whisker of the mouse.
The worm ate me,
then shot me out.
I was the rock and the sunlight.
I am the air breathing right now.

You know what?
I still am.
I am all these things still.

"Grandfather, the stars, they look back at me."
"No daughter, they are you,
you look at your reflection."

There are people moving up in the sky.
I know,
I sat and watched them.
They were sky people.
Not people who live in the sky,
they *were* the sky.
Do they know Rock Person?
There is a boulder in the meadow—
Rock Man.
Someone told me rocks were bones,
bones, earth bones.
But they're not, they're flesh,
they just move slower.

"Grandfather? Are there many, many people?"
"Huh? Yes! Yes, granddaughter, many."
"How many?"
"I don't know. Let's go get blackberries,
and lie on the meadow and eat them.
We can ask the grass people."

"Grandfather?"
"Yes, child."
"You comfort me, leaning here against you."

"Grandfather?"
"Yes."
"What do you do all day?"
"I stand, child.
I watch the stars dance,
I listen to the mist,
I see the sun high and pale in the sky."

"But Grandfather,
how do you see? You have no eyes or ears."
"I listen with my spirit, I see with my heart.
I've seen many things."

"Many, Grandfather? Show me."
"Lean against me, close your eyes.
What do you see?"
"I see a high meadow in the mountains
and a single standing tree."

"Look closely, in the tree's arms.
What is there?"
"A house, an eagle's house
with a single young eagle beating her wings on the wind,
learning to speak with the air."

"That child is you and me."
"You and me Grandfather?"
"We've known each other long, granddaughter."

"Grandfather, the ants have made a home in your feet
and are climbing in your bark."

"Lean your ear against me and listen.
What do you hear?"
"I hear the rain and a woodpecker."
"Listen, further away . . ."
"I hear an eagle singing."

"Yes, child, tomorrow talk to your Grandfather,
that big boulder there in the sun."

"All right, but Grandfather why am I here?"
"I called you, granddaughter,
I missed you,
your wings and my branches."

I was falling or flying.
I lay in my bed and fell up
through the roof of my cabin,
through the cloud people,
through the black.

"You know, Grandfather,
they didn't tell us everything in school.
They said the stars were only flaming balls of gas."

As I fell or flew,
I saw star people.
I fell through them.
People with long, silver, streaming hair

Old and powerful.
Watching.
Smiling and grim at the same time.
Some glanced at me and waved.

As I fell or flew, I couldn't decide which.
I fell and fell, on and on.
"I saw, Grandfather, what I can't say in words,
only in thoughts."
I flew and flew, then down, or was it up?
Through sky, through earth,
through the floor of my cabin
to my bed and sleeping bag.
One star had given me something.
As I lay, I opened my hand.
Light and Light, Grandfather.

Carry a feather into a dream.

The cabin door opened one afternoon.
The wolves heard someone.
They trotted out, then trotted back.

I went outside.
Golden light.
Tall tree people, holding up their arms.

A raven croaked.
By my jeep's door was a feather,
a raven's primary.
The ones that hold the wind.
Black. Light grey down.

The old man says,
"Carry this into your dreams."

I try, Grandfather, but it's hard for me to see
which is dream and which is real.

A man told me,
"That one cannot live here."
I say, "Which one?"
"That white one which stands beside you."
"Oh him! He's my teacher.
He goes where he wishes."

The man is confused,
"No, the other one which lies on your bed.
The grey one."
"Oh her, she's my sister.
I feed her till she can feed herself."
"You cannot give her this meat."
"Eh? This deer gave itself to us."
"She makes too much sound!"
"Oh? She is practicing her music.
Come sit and sing with us."

The man does not sit. He does not sing.
He says to us,
"You cannot keep her,
but she cannot be freed."

Teacher reaches up. He puts his paws
on the man's shoulders.
Teacher says, "Her people were here before
Coyote gave fire to the human beings.
The earth calls her, too. Listen."
The man sits down. He listens
He sings, like my sister.
"Oooowh Ooooooooowhhh!"

Prepare for the future,"
a man tells me and scurries away.
He scurries back. "You need this,
and this
and this
and this
and this
to prepare for the future."
He throws papers at me.
Ha! What does a wolf need with papers?
Coyote comes by. He takes a mouthful of papers.
"Hey, they're great to line a den with."

The man comes back.
"Well?" he says.
"What *is* the future?" I ask.
"It's this time up there!"
"What?"
He waves his hand, "Don't you see it? Up there!"
"No, I don't see it.
Only sky father, and the cloud persons, and sun person,
and the wind people."

Coyote comes back and yaps.
He grabs more papers and trots off.
"Well?" says the man.
"What do you see?"
He is tapping, tapping his foot.
He makes me nervous.

"Uh, I see this moment," I say.
Coyote comes back and sits watching us with yellow eyes.
(There are no eyes like Coyote's.)
"What!" says the man leaping up,
"This moment is too!
too! too!
too! short!"
He scurries off.

"Huh," says Coyote. He licks his whiskers and yawns!
"This moment is forever," says Coyote.
Then he starts howling and jogs off.

You know,
I can still hear him.
So it must be true.

Well then, the first man comes back.
He says, "Look behind you."
I look. I see the old deer trail through the trees.
"Well?" says the man.
"Uh? What?" I say.
"There's nothing there," says the man.
"No papers, paper clips, filing cabinets, digital watches."
"No," I say. "There aren't."

He looks at me importantly.
"You've got no past," he grimaces.
"You are unimportant, a no account person."
He holds out a paper.
"This has my picture here and a story." He shows me.
"See, this and this and this, dates of important things."
"I see where the ant people
or maybe a muddy chickadee has walked."
"Ha!" he says.
Coyote comes by. "Show me," he says.
The man shows him.
Coyote snaps it up in his mouth.
"Perfect," says Coyote. "The finishing touch!
I'm building a nest for the new world.
Pups are messy; this will absorb the shit."

that same day!

A woman comes up to me and grabs my arm.
"Your jeans are torn."
"Oh that. Well, Blackberry Bush was playing with me.
She wanted a piece of my clothes for luck."
"Whaaaat!" The woman says, "Well, your hair is a mess."
"No, it's not. Wind styled it just this morning," I say.
"NO! You must have your hair and clothes like this,
and this
and this'
and this."
Coyote came by and said, "Woman,
your husband just went that way."
The woman said, "Whaaat!" And ran off.

"Let's go swimming," says Coyote.
"I'll style your hair."

I left the
wood burning stove open
and Smoke came in.
Smoke in the corner
waving,
dancing.

I talked to him.
"Come closer?" I asked.
Smoke said softly,
"If I come closer,
you won't be able to see me."
"Oh," I said.

Smoke fingered my notebook.
"I like your poetry."
The pages fluttered.
"But really very little about Smoke."
"Are you a helper to me?"
"No, just an acquaintance.
Though I do carry your prayers
and chase certain things.
I move between the worlds."

"Will you give me wisdom?"
Smoke laughed softly.
"I already have.

"Write me a poem," Smoke said.
Then he squeezed out a crack in the wall.
I later saw my notebook was smudged.

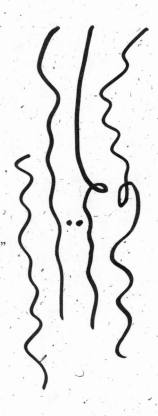

As I leaned against Brother,
I saw something under the branches where I sat.
It was like a house in there.
Brother was sheltering me.

I saw this.
The branches in front of me wove themselves into a wreath
and dancing, they circled.

Brother moved up higher and higher;
and I sat leaning against the trunk.

Then through the branches I saw
(as if the first wasn't enough)
the universe, peering.
The gaps between branches became stars,
galaxies, all dancing.
The branches became the black in between.

I leaned against Brother, hard.
I didn't want to fall from Brother
and spin off who knows where.

Then the Brother was back where we started.
I blinked,
unsure if I was having a vision or losing my mind.
I never did drugs. I'm glad, who needs them.
The world is confusing enough.

"You're tired," I say to myself.
"Yes," says Brother, "you're tired."
"Yes," says Coyote as he trots by.
Coyote is carrying something in his mouth,
is burying something next to Brother.
It looks like a small sun.

Sometimes these mysteries are confusing,
all the time for me.
Rabbit laughs at this and rolls around on the ground.

Have you met old Rabbit?
Sometimes he's an old man in a red plaid shirt and jeans.
Sometimes a young man with his face painted half white,
half black.

He says everything opposite.
Though sometimes as an old man,
when I'm really confused by his words,
he says things straight
(though he never did this when I first met him).

When I met him, he was sitting on a red roan horse
backwards, humming a little song.
I was trying to find my way out of a dream.
It was on open ground, sage growing and littlest oaks.
Summer.
Morning.

I ask him,
"Why are you sitting on your horse backwards?"
He looks at me with a face half black, half white.
"I'm not sitting backwards."
"Yes you are."
"No, you're wrong."
"Well, who are you?"
"I'm a great warrior!"
He sticks out his chest.
The red roan begins grazing.

"You don't look like one," I say.
"What's your name?"
"Rabbit!" he says proudly.
"Rabbit? That's not a warrior's name."
"Yes it is," he frowns down at me,
"It is a great fierce name."
He scowls, tossing his long hair back.

"Well I have to go now," I say.
He says, "I'll show you how I scalp people."
"What!" I say. "No, I don't want to see that."
"No you don't," he says.
We walk off together, he riding backwards.
Rabbit giggling softly.

We come to some people sleeping in a tent.
Normal people?
Rabbit gets off his horse and crawls backwards
up to the people.
He has a long knife.

Oh no!
He takes their shoes, then carefully peels off their socks,
crawls back and hangs them on a stick.
Looks at me proudly.
"Ha!" he says.

The next time I saw Rabbit, he was old,
sitting in a little grassy valley.
I was talking with him.
I was barefoot,
my hair loose.

I was standing a little ways off.
Rabbit looked at me
a long, slow glance.

Rabbit pointed at a high, far off mountain
and I kept walking.
I knew that was my path.
Rabbit looked at me a long time as I walked away.
I could feel his old eyes on me.

As I went on I felt
the wolves trotting behind,
the breath of the mountain on my face,
the grass under my feet.

Once I saw an old prison.
There was a cage,
flattened iron bars, very small.
Rabbit was sitting in there,
no room to stand, none to lie down.
It was very hot.

I said to the man who walked up,
"What are you doing to this person?"
Rabbit looked at me from one white eye, one black.
"You are very cruel to do this," I said.

The man said,
"That old Coyote, he's crazy,
you just move along, ma'am."
I said to Rabbit, "What are you going to do?"
"Well," said Rabbit,
"I think *you* should worry and be very afraid.
I'm very weak."
Then slowly Rabbit became Coyote.
The man who stood watching said,
"Hey where's the prisoner?" and opened the cage door.
The Coyote ran out, yapped at me to follow and ran away.

Jim asked once to ask Rabbit if he was like Coyote.
I did.
Rabbit grinned.
"Coyotes, what are they?"
"I don't like them," he answered.

I was going on vision quest high in the mountains,
among the tall, thin pine people.

I was sitting, thinking.
I hope Brother Grizzly doesn't come here,
for I'm sworn not to leave this spot.

Then I heard the crash of brush,
the grumbling groan of Grizzly Man coming fast.
Sworn to stay! Hell!
I ran like mad! Brother Grizzly right behind.

When I could no longer run, I turned.
Grizzly stopped and slowly became old Rabbit,
who sat on the ground and laughed till he cried.
Rolling.

I had one long dream, I think.
I think I'm still having it.
I was with old Rabbit in the open, plains.
Rabbit didn't talk.

"Why am I here?" I asked.
"Rabbit wants you to dance a circle for sometime,"
said a small white stone at Rabbit's feet.
"Dance the sun up and down through the night and day.
But you must come willingly, for when you start
there is no stopping, no waking up."
"No waking up," I said. "I am dreaming now."
I looked at old Rabbit, who sat smoking,
and he smiled at me.

The stone said, "Try to wake yourself."
I tried, I couldn't.
Imagine trying to wake yourself when you're not dreaming.
That's how it felt.
I was frightened and struggled to wake.

Then I was awake in my old cabin, in my sleeping bag,
the wolves watching me.

Grandfather, what a price I am paying,
grieving over one who is my sister, now not seen.
She would run before me, joyful,
then turn and look; still coming, you!

I taught her how to take life for food,
life for living. I had to honor these ones.
I cannot go back,
I cannot see her captive, yet now I cannot see her.

Do you understand, Grey One?
Did you choose? I wonder.
I left you and I feel like you're betrayed.
But I'm betrayed.

We are neither one thing nor the other.
I envy you your journey,
though it may be short.
I wish I could follow, I did see wolf sign.
Please find your family,
please find your food,
please find your life and sing;
sing for the one in the cabin who couldn't come.

Grandfather walks.
He comes to me and we look out into the grey.
We see
wolves,
wolves
then only trees.

These voices,
these powers,
these people,
I'm going to send you all to Penny directly.
Tell her your secrets, directly to her typewriter.

Grandfather laughs, seeing this,
"The office is too small to hold these ones
that live inside my heart."

Yet Penny catches them on her typewriter,
and hey!
No escape, you powers.

Penny steps outside for a moment away from her typewriter,
and when she comes back,
well hey, there's Coyote on the counter,
and old Rabbit reading a magazine.
A great tree has grown through the window
and wolves lie panting on the floor.

Penny didn't understand when she took this job
that these would come.
Eagle chirps at her from the back of an old chair.
Coyote and Rabbit soon are arguing
about where their words go.

Penny asks them to come back much later,
but they don't budge.

Soon Brenda from the appraisal company
comes in to make copies,
but she can't get the ocean off the copier.
No room too small or too big,
Penny sighs and types.

One morning I woke and sensed you calling
and so we came in the red jeep, Cherry.

Stormy, tall, grey clouds thick with rain,
the sea was falling on the northern mountains.
The signs said, "Road Closed."
The men said, "You cannot go there.
Avalanches," they said.
So I became invisible and hiked in anyway.
They couldn't hear you calling.

The ground *was* very uneasy.
Never have I seen such power in the Little Waters.
I asked them for strength,
and the trees and rocks for guidance,
as Grandfather had taught me.

Once, Peter the timber wolf stopped.
His hair lifted and his eyes fixed on me.
He told me. I knew!
We all ran and the ground slid behind us.
I left that place a lock of my hair,
and asked the mountains to wait till I found you.
They did. I could feel them holding themselves.

The waters had risen to the base of the bridge.
We all stopped at the end
and decided not to look at the waters
as we crossed the slender planks, shaking.

When we got to the other creek, I was stumped.
I knew you were calling but I didn't want to get
caught in hungry water.
Again, Peter looked at me, ran at the creek and jumped.
Of course he looked very nice.
I looked rather silly when I did it, hands clutching at the bank,
Peter wuffing softly.
Then there you were waiting.
Did the others send you back?

So happy were we all, that on the return,
we didn't notice the ten miles.
The pouring rain, which sang in a million voices of its power.
The quivering earth.

The road was gone when Cherry took us back.
But we got across and waved at the men who were angry
because we wouldn't obey signs,
only follow voices.

grasses
coming

I hear someone calling,
a voice I know.
I hear, yet I see no one.
The voice is soft, gentle, low, sweet.
The voice of a mother,
the voice of a woman.
"What do you want?
Where are you?"

I'm in the cabin with Grandfather,
sitting by the wood stove.
The rain is coming down.

I ask Grandfather, who sits with his back to the stove,
his eyes closed, facing east,
"How do I find that one, Grandfather?"
Grandfather says to me,
"Hey, what you do is you follow that voice.
You answer.
What else do you do when someone calls?"

So I go out to the rain and I listen.
Soon I hear calling, sad, sweet.
She calls my secret name,
the one Grandfather says is only for me
and the powers to know.
How does she know?
I follow,
east,
south,
west,
north,
all around.
I look to the sky,
I see no one calling.
I go to the meadow,
to the circle of trees and sit.
Coyote trots up.
"Eh, what are you doing?"

"I'm trying to follow a voice."
"Oh ho, that one. You are looking wrong," says Coyote.
I look at him. He smiles.
"Eh, daughter, put your ear to the ground."

One day in Southland,
I and the grey horse
went up to the center of the world.
Brother let me sit on his back and he carried me up.
On the thin trail, in the sage and oaks and granite people,
I heard someone crying.
We looked.
In the brush lay a hawk woman.
Someone had hurt her.
She lay crying, lifting her great wings and unable to fly.
I jumped down from my brother and gathered her up.
"I'll take you to Grandfather. He'll heal you."
It was hard to get back on Brother's back, but I did,
and Hawk lay still against my chest,
her eyes still watching the sky.

I took her to Grandfather,
who talked to her.
Then Grandfather said to me,
"Her spirit is very light now.
She wants to go to Grandmother's arms."
We sat with Hawk till she had gone to Grandmother.
I went outside and sent my tears with her.

When I went to the mountain later,
a great hawk landed very close to me.
She looked in my face and laughed softly.
As she lifted away,
a single red feather from her bustle dropped
and fell to the new grass.
I got off Brother and picked it up,
thinking of that one flying in Grandmother's lands.

One morning in my seventh summer, I think,
I came up the path from Old Lake Woman to the cabin.
Fish had given themselves to me,
for me and Father's morning meal.

As I struggled up the hill,
something swooped low over my head,
then another something.
I looked up. My breath stopped.
Eagles were circling over me, many gold eagles.
I was very afraid.
They were big, powerful, holy.
I was only a little girl with many fish.
I left the eagles my fish and ran up the hill.

The eagles followed me,
I could see Father watching from the cabin.
I was very afraid and ran to Father's arms.
He said nothing.

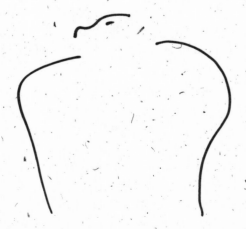

Sometimes when I'm sad
the trees sing to me,
the grass cries with me.
If I watch long enough,
will I understand?

In my dreams I travel light.
I wish to travel that light on this side.
In my dreams I make no tracks,
my feet do not leave their mark
on the face of the earth.
I have no shadow.

I want to learn to walk that way here,
on this side.
In the center of the world, I picked nothing.
I took nothing.
Soon the small stones called to me,
"Sister take us."
And the sage sang out,
"You need us."
So I took one small white stone and four stems of sage.
I gave a lock of my hair.

I left that country.
I don't think I'll see it again.

A person once said to me,
"Ah, someone is talking through you."
I looked at my reflection in the pond.
Coyote and Grandfather watched.
"No, it's me talking."

I took Grandfather to town once.
In a store a man talked to him so fast
Grandfather couldn't understand him.
He was trying to get us to buy something.
Something we couldn't live without,
something that saves time and energy.

I told Grandfather what he meant.
Grandfather coughed.
He was embarrassed for the man,
that the 'man had so little time that he needed to save it,
so little strength he needed to store it.

Grandfather said to the man,
"Eh, oh, we live with many persons,
we have much help.
We don't need this thing."
Then we went home,
to the cabin and the wolves.

The heat makes the air dance.
The wolves' singing makes my heart dance.
The snow people, when they fall,
all dance in spiraling circles.
The wind always asks others to dance.
"Grandfather, what a lot of dancing!"
"Ho, yes daughter,
you know everything in balance
dances its life."

A man once came to the cabin
and asked me to ask my Grandfather the name of a bird.
The man described what the bird looked like.
Grandfather got up, hearing us speaking
and opened the cabin door wide.

Sunlight fell in and the wolves fell out.
The man took a few backward steps.
Grandfather came to him
and put his hand on the man's arm.
He looked into the man's eyes.
Grandfather said, "Grandson, I don't know.
You must speak with the bird."

This dreaming is hard,
hard to explain,
hard to understand.
So real it is
to taste,
to feel,
to smell,
to see,
to hear,
in this land of my dreams.
Why, the inside of my head is one huge country
where I, a traveler, explore.

One time I sat on a high hill,
one of my teachers beside me,
in a cold treeless land,
the sky the color of mule deer's back.
My teacher said, "Look below, what do you see?"
Below was a great tribe,
breath visible in the cold wind.
I said to my teacher, "I see the caribou people."
He said, "You will choose the one we hunt,
the one who calls us. Which?"

I looked at the people who slowly walked.
At the end of the group limped an old great one,
his head low, but beautiful.
He glanced up at us.
His eyes fixed on my face for a moment.
His breath held for a heartbeat.

"This one," I said to the teacher.
"This is true," he answered.
"You must strike the throat and take his life.
I will only help."

We trotted off down the hill
and with the easy grace of my people,
ran toward this tribe.
They also ran.
Quickly this happened,
but also slowly.
I could feel the brittle grasses under my feet.
My lungs filled with very cold wind.
My teacher drew the old one from his herd.
Their spirits sang once to him as his people galloped on.

As we neared and my teacher grasped the old one's flank,
growling at me to kill,
I leaped at his throat and was kicked
and stumbled at the old one's side as he fell.

I could hear him praying, "Thank you,
my death is honorable to teach this young one.
Come! I go, but come once more."
I grasped his throat.
A great horror and sadness but also reverence
came to my spirit
as I tasted his blood
and he died.

My teacher opened him swiftly and we ate.
Then we sat down on the earth,
feeling the brittle grass under our paws,
seeing a wide cold sky.
We pointed our noses to the face of the father
and sang to the spirit of our brother.

When I came back from Grandmother's land, that night,
my body became sick and hot.
I lay in my sleeping bag in my cabin,
the wolves around me.
I lay sick all night, crying to be well again.

My fire died in the wood burning stove.
The morning came slowly, the grey, cold morning.
I lay sick, no fire.
The cabin door opened, a few people came in.
I could hardly raise my head to look at them.
They wore tule grass slippers and capes of rabbit fur,
men and women, faces decorated with lines.
Proud, strong, dark, short people, they came in.

One came to my bed. The wolves saw him and did nothing.
He lay his hand on my face.
"Chu, chu," he said. "Lie still.
You have come from a land that is dying
and some of that dying has entered your body
and made you sick."

I could only stare at him. Then he said,
"I will take this sickness from your body."
He took out a tule reed, put it to my neck
and sucked on the end.
A woman standing next to him held a bowl
which the man spat into.
It looked like tar.

I felt better after this and rose up to look around.
One of the women had re-lit the wood stove
and was adding wood.
The man said, "My name is Grasses Coming.
I'll ask you a question: How can we live outside,
dressed as we are,
and never become sick?"

I said I didn't know.
"I'll tell you," he said, "Because the land wasn't sick then.
The people made the land sick.
Then the land couldn't care for them
so the people became sick."

He saw a packet of flu medicine by my bed,
he took a tablet out and tasted it.
He looked at me. "This is poison," he said.
"It makes the body
think it is well, when it's not.
True medicine helps the body heal itself,
not make the body think it's well, when it isn't.
Then the sickness does not leave."

"How do you know me?" I asked him.
"We've watched you long,
from the center of the world,
where Coyote first created the earth.
We watched a child play on the mountain.
You honored our stories.
You honored our trees and sacred spots.
Eh, we like you. We come a long way to you, to heal you.
Your name should be in our way of speaking."
I dreamed of a wolf, or wolf dreaming.
"I, I am Grasses Coming. We will watch you."
I awoke some time later feeling better, my house warm.
Grasses Coming.

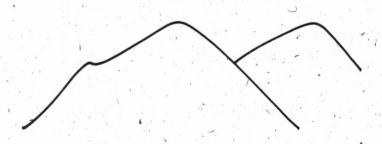

To Corrymeela

Grandfather.
My Mother.
Powers.
Can't you stop this war?"

"We could,
but you've all decided."

"I don't understand."

"Child, you've said it yourself,
the way the horse thinks,
the way a gathering of fish swim.
One turns, they all turn."

I hear them calling at night, the travelers.
They call as they fly through night land over my cabin,
breathless, but calm,
a little sad, perhaps, but free.
They call to one another,
"We're all together, we're all together,
Mother,
Father,
Sister,
Brother."
On and on they call, through all their relatives.
They call to me as they fly, I think.
"Cousin! Cousin, you can hear us so we're calling you.
Do we make you feel lighter, as we call?
Can you feel the wind of your cousins pull at your wings?"
I call back, "Yes! Yes cousins!"
I dance in the circle of trees,
arms out, twirling, hair loose.
Under the rivers of light, silver grey,
light like Grandfather's hair,
I dance,
I dance with the snow geese.

Standing in slow swinging surf,
looking at the sea's long rollers,
blue,
blue, green?
"Grandfather, what's this color?"
"Child, ask the one who belongs to it."

I swam out and out,
my arms and the sea's foam laughing.
The fish thought I was a cloud person.
I dove. I heard fish talk.
"Grandfather, I cannot understand these fish people."
I rose again.
"Granddaughter, must you understand everything?"

Then I heard a voice, not Grandfather.
Soft, low, the sound,
big, gentle.
"Come."
So I swam, out and out.
"Come."
I sat at the waves' tops, in the arms of this teacher.
Breathe.
The waves touch the lava far away.
Breathe.,
The waves sound endless.
Breathe.
Straight down, many heartbeats.
"Grandfather, look at me diving."
No answer. Grandfather is watching a whale breach in seas
cold, far away. Down and down.
Coral like flowers.

Fish follow me.
I reach the forest top and look out,
straight into the deep blue,
"Grandfather? Blue, green?"
Grandfather doesn't answer. He is talking to a child far away.

The sea lifts and carries.
Breathes in and out.
Surf against the rocks and down the sand.
"Who are you?" I say, "What is this color?"
Laughter, deep.
"Well, eh. What name? It's you, diver."

Up and up, towards the clearing sea,
fish chase my feet and laugh.
At the air world I breathe.
"Grandfather, a voice down there!"
"Daughter, all around you."

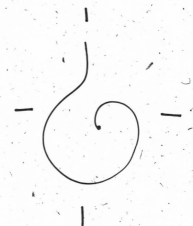

I saw a man in a white coat.
He stood in a meadow.
He was looking, looking,
at a fox skull,
peering in eye holes, peering in ear holes,
turning, turning. "Hum! What's this then?"

Coyote jogged up.
"What are you doing?" asked Coyote.
"Studying." The man drew himself up.
Two foxes came up behind to watch.
The coons brought their families.
Chickadee said, "We know, know, know a story
about that, that fox."
The man didn't hear. He broke the skull in pieces.
"This way I can label it and know it,"
he said. He saw no one.

Coyote shrugged and squinted and smiled.
"Who can argue with such a one," said Coyote.
Coyote then trotted off tra, tra, tra
to talk about lunch with the foxes.

Grandfather, the little hurt ones,
the lost ones. They come to me."
Grandfather smiles.
"Why, Grandfather?"
"Maybe you were cold,
and the wolf shared her coat with you.
Or hungry and the deer fed you.
Maybe sad and the little dancing fox made you smile.

"Now you share your warmth, your food, your dancing."
"But Grandfather, I'm sad to see them go."
"Not tears to see them leave you, but wishes for
food
warmth
dancing.
Next time you'll go first."

Sparrow came. He looked at me.
I asked him, "Where will I go?"
"North!
North!"
"And my sister?"
"North!
North!"
"And my brother?"
"North!
North!"
"Why?" I asked Sparrow Man.
Sparrow said as he fluffed his wings
and stretched out each foot slowly,
"I don't know."
"Closer, come closer, little brother."
"No, I don't get much closer than this to anyone,
unless we are married.
It's my way."
He lifted away.
A little bird told me
"North!
North!"

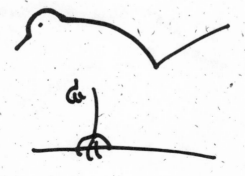

There is one who is not free.
She gave herself the life of a servant
or is it a sister?
Who out of love needs no one else but me.

She has stood between horn and hoof.
She has bled for me, cried, sung and played.

Once I asked her to bite a drunk who angered me.
But she, in wisdom, would not.
Yet when I was alone and afraid of someone,
she was unafraid and stood between us
crying, "No!
No!"

You have followed me for a long while.
I hope when this is over you follow me to spirit place
spirit home
spirit woman
spirit hound.

I came home.

"Grandfather, I brought candles for your birthday."
Grandfather wasn't there, so I lit one candle.
Staring at the flame, I heard its heart speak.
"I see blue," Flame said, "when I look into your face.
The color blue."
"I see yellow," I said, "when I look at you.
You are beautiful, perfect heat and light."
"You too are beautiful in quite another way."
"What do you see when you look at me?" I asked.
"Blue, the color blue," said the flame,
"and a human being, a person."
"Are all flames the same?"
"No daughter, we are all separate,
many different kinds of fire, you know.
But we are all one part of the whole spirit of fire."
"Oh,
you are dying now."
"Yes, but this moment has been forever for me."
"Will I see you again?"
"Yes, when you are very old on your last day.
You will look and see me reborn
and remember this time.
Write a poem about me."
I turned to get a paper.
When I turned back Flame was gone
and the birthday candle was a small pool of wax
on the old wooden table.

One time I dreamed myself an old great grandma,
skinny, wrinkled, sitting before a fire
within a circle of my family.
Summer, clear night, cedar smoke.

My great grandkids asked me for an old time story,
but not this time about Coyote.
About the false men who made war on our mother.
"What was it like, Granny?"
(They were astonished at my remembering.)
"It was very strange," I said.
"Every one of the false people
kept a lot of things, but never gave them away.
They were immortal, always looked like kids.
Strange, eh?
And too thin. Wouldn't last the winter.
They were afraid of the earth, didn't like to touch it.
Yet they were a dirty people.
Believe it or not, they were afraid of themselves.

"Finally they ate each other up
and we, the true people,
fled to these mountains.
We went back and prayed.
And you know, Coyote came back
and gave us fire and other things again."

The Grey One and I went to the mountains
because in my dreams I saw
a pack waiting for us.

The men told me she wouldn't learn to kill.
I brought her her first live food,
as I'm sure her white mother would have.
She remembered.
They told me the pack would kill her,
but in my dream, the pack waited gently for her.

The men said when she was grown, she'd attack me.
We play this game.
I put my hand behind her great fangs
and we walk around, attached,
fang to hand.

I see her mother in my mind,
pacing, innocent, trapped.
Her pleading eyes.
When I let the Grey One go free
she stayed by me, licking my face, playing.

The wolves wuff softly.
I step outside.
"What is it, Grandfather?"

I see the clouds,
the moon with shadows of a rainbow.
They shine through the hole in the sky.

All the universe looks at me through that hole
and says,
"Come,
come."
"Come where, Grandfather?"
"Come to us,
step through,
step across.
If you won't come to us, we'll come to you."

I want to go back, Grandfather.
I don't understand this new way."

A man gave me a job stuffing paper into more paper.
"What is this for?"
"Why! For more paper."
"What do people do with all this paper?"
"They throw it away."
"Where does this paper come from?"
"Oh those things out there."
"What things?"
"Those green things, the tree people."
"Oh, uh, yes."

I quit that job and went back to the cabin.
Grandfather laughed when he saw me.

The sky fingers came down one day
and walked around doing nothing
but ruffling the village of grasses.
Rattled my windows, fluffed the wolves,
then left to find the arm hole in the robe of the world.

I threw an old piece of wood on my fire.
Too late I saw mushrooms growing there.
As they burned, I told them I was sorry.
Their tiny voices shouted out strong,
breathless,
happy.
"Never mind," they said. "We'll see *you* later!"

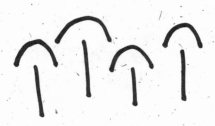

The grey mist stalks the trees
like the Grey One stalks rabbits.
Golden eyes
misted fur
her legs move
her back doesn't
head low
ears flat
close to the earth she stalks.
Wolf and mist.
The mist hides the Grey One
and the Grey One breathes mist.

The woman who waits with the herons
said to me,
"I am very sad,
what will happen?
These lost ones will kill us all,
all the true people."

Coyote came up to us
and whispered to me.

I said to this woman,
"Maybe these lost ones'
grip on our mother
will become so loose
they'll spin off in the blackness,
up with the star people and float around.
And then we'll wave and shout,
'Hold onto each other.' "
Then we'll all go with Coyote
and have a big dance.

to the one who gave me horses

Your footsteps fade
into the long grass.
The sky is darkened.

We hear your call no more.

The stars turn from behind
the clouds.
The sun comes.
We remember
the glance, the hand's caress,
the dear face and noble mind.

I had seen the falcon.
He sped across the sky,
light over his wings.
He rode the wind.

The sun and moon
have turned many times
and my spirit doesn't cry your name.

I understand you rode the wind
as the falcon.
I rode the earth
with the horses.

The horses, Father, were your
gift of life to me.
I know now
hey, we'll meet again.
On the narrow trail,
the trail following
the sunset path.

By the circle of trees
are many tall leafless people.
It is winter.
They stand near the pond.
The wolves and I
ran by one day
and these people called to me.
I stopped and listened to them.
They sang together.
Then sometimes one among them would speak.
"We're frightened, but we do not run.
We have great fear, but we face it with peace.
We turn and stand,
our hands gripping our grandmother's flesh,
our hands holding our grandfather's body.
What will happen, Tsimmu?
Eh? What do you think?"
I said, "I don't know."
"We wait, we'll stand here and wait."
"I will wait too," I said.

"Tell the others what we think,
what we think, what we say,
we the Alder People,
that's what they call us."

Twister came down
dancing across the grass.
Twister came down
lifted the dust and
fingered the leaves.

The black colt watched.
Twister waited for me.
I walked up
close,
closer to see Twister dance.

Twister laughed, danced, disappeared.
Hey, just vanished.
I stared around looking,
looking.
So did the black colt.

(However, the wolves were asleep.)
Then Twister came back.
Hey, right over the top of me!
My shirt flapped,
my hair swirled with Twister.
I danced,
I danced,
I danced,
with Twister.

I walked to a hill
and looked down,
down to the low grassland.
The place is where many wild ones lived.
Now I see the docile cattle eating,
eating.

I was sad thinking of the wild ones.
who once ran here.

Grandmother tapped me on my arm.
She had been behind me, silent.

"Granddaughter, do you understand,
do you know?
Hey, daughter,
if I call these docile ones,
they will all come back to me.
Hair will grow long,
horn will be sharp,
eyes will glitter,
calves will jump and buck
if I call them.
Hey daughter, look at you."

My bones know
my bones know
my bones know
something
something that the inside of my head
doesn't know.

My bones say
trust us.
My bones say
follow us.

My bones are old
very old
old.
They are older than the inside of my head.

My bones know
who is lying in the brush.
My bones know
where the spring runs.
The wild people,
the free ones
can see that my bones know.
They see I trust my bones.
They also follow their bones.

My bones will lie by themselves one day,
by themselves under the sky people.
Dry bones,
they will tell all they know
to the sky and earth.
They will tell all they know to the people
who come to find them.
They will speak,
speak to all, if left free.

My bones know
my bones know
my bones know
something.

Grandfather, what is a vision?"
"This is, daughter."
"All this?"

"Grandfather, I saw something."
"Eh daughter, did your bones tell you?!"
"Oh my Grandfather! You're laughing."
Grandfather's face becomes still.
"What did you see?"

"A plain between two circles
of great mountains.
A place where the grass is very tall,
the grass people very happy.
In this place were many horses,
many beautiful horses.

"And standing on the mountain sides
were many, many people,
all watching. From down the mountains
came wolves.
The wolf people ran down the sides of the mountains.
They ran in with all the horses
and then they all ran together.
Together they ran up the sky
like Twister Person does.
They swirled together and ran up the sky.
The people were happy.
The mountains smiled.

"What does it say Grandfather?"
Grandfather gets up off his stool,
he looks out the cabin window
into the circle of trees.
"Ask your bones, daughter."

I dreamed,
I thought I dreamed
nursing from my mother,
her white fur,
her tongue caressing me,
her small sounds,
her warmth,
the roundness and softness
of her belly.

She began to become something.
Something else,
something more,
bigger and bigger.
She grew, spreading.
Then I awoke.

I had fallen asleep on the rounded meadow,
among the circle of trees.
My hands gripped the grass
and my face pressed against her flesh.

When I walk in the circle of trees,
I say hello to all there,
the ones seen,
the ones I don't see.

They all know my secret name,
they all greet me.
I say, "How do you know my name?"
They say, "Hey you, you have many names."
"Dark Hair!"
"The one who runs with wolves"
"The one who is alone"
"The one who dances strangely"
"Oh you! So what are all your names then?"
"Eh? We! We are called The People."

Always,
always I feel them.
They move like a steady wind
that blows across the grasses.

I ride the old stallion.
His feet make a drumbeat prayer
on the earth.

He is like the old man elk.
His thinking is always on his wives
and his place.

He lets me ride him in the mountains.
He lets the wolves run with him.
The wolves follow us,
floating loosely above the trail
the way,
the way wolves go.

The sky I stare at,
the father, the grandfather,
the mother, the grandmother,
the powers, the earth.

I must stare. I can't see it enough.
It is so clear.
I must watch a long time.
I can hear the sea,
my old friend.

We follow the narrow trail down
to the open.
We all then feel the calling.
We turn and run,
this moment together,

There is no time,
there is no difference between us,
the stallion, the wolves, the woman.

I see Grandmother in the circle of trees.
One time I sit
and talk with her.

I'd seen this story.
I tell her about people in another place,
dusty,
hot.

I saw them walking,
like antelope, they walked.
Their skin tight, dark,
their limbs like carved wood.
Beautiful
to be like them,
tall,
antelope people.

I laugh, I show her
how they walk.
But it is not the same.
I'm not quite like them.
(You see, I'm lighter.
I'm wolf.)
Grandmother, she laughs!

The story tells how these beautiful ones
are unhappy.
It is hard to describe.
I see oceans coming together in anger,
green,
blue,
black water.
Roaring angry.

I say, "Granny, why is this?"
She says, "I don't know, daughter.
As the life blood of the world
runs equal under all the land,
so does the blood of all life run equal.
None of my children are the same."

She pauses and looks long at me.
"The same is sickness you know."

I look again at the angry oceans.
Something changes,
the waters calm.
They flow together,
black, blue, green,
where they touch rainbows
of ocean water.

Grandmother laughs and walks away from me.
She wades in the earth
like a heron in water.
Her laugh becomes the wind,
cool, soft.

what grandfather told ann

"Grandfather, this place is sad."
Yes, daughter, it is.
"Then how do I walk here?"
Look!
See how the deer step.
Watch the birds in the sky father's arms.

Think back.
You'll feel the wolves breathe in the fog,
the bear claws mark the clay.
You'll see how the people rejoice
in the sacredness of the trees
and how they mourn the passing
of their loved ones.
Treat this place as if your
people were buried here in the sky.
When you walk,
each plant and tree will bless you,
and you'll find yourself
walking as a deer.
Step, step,
pause,
look, breathe!
At peace with this place.

One night I went to bed
in my cabin,
in my sleeping bag.
When I woke,
the world had changed.
I had been dreaming.
I woke in a different house
made of the skin of
"the one who gives everything to us."

My bed was made from his hide,
thick, warm.
I was much younger.
My brothers, sisters slept around me.
My mother and father too.
I woke and told
my mother and father,
"I've had a strange dream
about another place."
As I told them of where I had dreamed,
I heard my father's horses outside,
dogs barking around the places
of our family who lived about us.

I was glad the other was a dream.
Grandfather moved and stood up from his night place.
He stared at me and pointed outside.
Mother and father were silent.
I went outside.
The sun was walking up the
great bones of the mountains.
On the closest hill
sat a white wolf.
She was calling.
I went towards her
and many steps later,
I awoke once more in my cabin.
The Grey One was sleeping next to me,
the cabin very still.

Rabbit, I know you can make it rain."
"No, I can't."
"Why do you say everything backwards?"
"Ha it is you! You're the one."
"Rabbit, make it rain."
"Yes, it is snowing already."
"You make no sense."
"No, I don't. Listen, deaf one.
Hey, hey, hey, laa, laa, laa, hoh hoh, hey."
He dances a bit wildly and a small twister comes,
like the ones that chase the leaves.

Rabbit stares with surprise, then begins chasing it,
running backwards.

"I'm a frightened one, Power. I'm weak and foolish."

Rabbit and Twister run off leaving me standing alone
on a wide plain up to my knees in grasses, dreaming.

This horse won't go. He won't jump.
He's a stubborn one. He's a stupid one, they said.
I looked at that horse standing in the dust.
He looked at me.
I slipped my rope over his head. He nodded his consent.
I said out loud to this horse,
"Hey, this fence is so small
you can jump it from a standstill."
The horse stamped his foot,
so we jumped it from the standstill.
You know? Now that horse is never in that place.
He jumps out.
He's over at my cabin, talking with Grandfather.

There is one who watches me.
Says nothing, watches, knowing.
He never speaks.
He is peaceful and a bit sad.
He kneels on the earth,
one knee touching, the other just bent.
As if he is ready to get up at any time,
but chooses not to.

He wears little clothing, nothing decorative,
not even a feather in his long black hair.
Who is this one?
How can I get him to speak?
Come, dream person,
come and have breakfast,
you and me and the wolves.

Grandfather, I'm sad."
"Ah! daughter look at the sunrise,
the laughing young sun.
See how he smiles at you from across the little pond.
Old Man Eagle wakes and is calling."

"But Grandfather, I'm foolish."
Grandfather skips on one leg.
"Oh then, look at the high ones, the old ones
holding their hands up through the cloud people.
They wear cold, white hats.
They breathe frost from their nose
and rake the ground with strong feet."

"Grandfather, I'm afraid."
"So now walk the sunset path into the night world.
Where owl is.
Look, daughter, deep into the night home
and see Old Man Grizzly,
who lives with himself, knows and is content."

"I'm so weary, Grandfather."
"Daughter, so many complaints. Come into the day.
See the green, rest with your mother,
watch Coyote dancing,
tricking the young mice and your heart into peace."
"But Grandfather, Coyote eats the mice."
"Yes, hum? So he does."
Grandfather scratches and stumps away, smiling.

That Old Rabbit, he gave me a trick,
as a present, as a power, as a medicine.
I managed in my dreams
to bring him the feather of a falcon.
I was so proud.

I found Rabbit that time as an old man sitting, smoking.
He slowly raised his eyes to mine, squinted.
But he was calm, serious.
I handed him my feather.
"Here, a present for you."
By the time it went from my hand to his,
it had changed to a ball point pen.
A rather nice one.
My face changed, as the feather did, to surprise.
Rabbit fell apart,
falling over, rolling,
laughing, laughing.

Next time I saw him, he was wearing it in his hair,
point down, like a feather.

I walked far into the brush one day,
and my hair hanging down was held by Blackberry Bush.
I said, "Grandmother Bush, do not take too much, eh."
Blackberry said nothing.

When I returned to the cabin, I found on my sleeve
a branch of blackberry, green leaves.
I put it in the window.
Thank you,
thank you, Grandmother Bush.

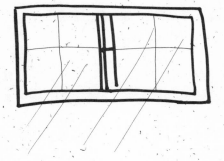

Grandfather, are you still there?"
I'm always here, Granddaughter.
"Grandfather, how many spirit powers are there?"
Only one, granddaughter.
Many voices, but one vision.
"One, Grandfather, but then how many people?"

One only, daughter.
Of all that there is in these lands,
the spirits and the people.
The Spirit and the Person.

I'm with you, daughter, and all that come after.
All that went before are with me.
We watch.
See yourself in the other people,
see all, in the world.

When you speak to
wolf
or
hawk
or
tree,
they speak with you, they are you.
I talk through them,
they speak to me of you.
We are the same.
When you look deeply into another living one's eyes,
you see yourself.
That is your gift, my daughter,
to see that you live inside all.
And that all live and see themselves in you.

When you kill for food,
you are taking of yourself.
Then do so in a holy way.
When you feed your fire,
understand that you give it yourself.
Do so in a holy way.
When you see the small birds in the snow,
know that you are they.
Watch in a holy way.
Do this for your joy.

Why, daughter, the air is holy and magic.
Everything sings for all people
of the joy of the great mystery.
This gives you a way of being
that is happiness and binding.
Remember I love you, daughter.
I am here always, daughter.

Mother,
my Mother,
you are far away on your path,
and I'm here on my path,
you in Grandmother's country
and I in Northland.

You gave me a brush for my hair when I last saw you.
Now far away, I brush my hair
and see your grey hairs
mingled with my black ones.

The is a void,
a breaking of the circle,
a bundle of sage tossed away.
I see the great grassland,
my relatives crying,
don't forget us,
don't forget us,
we're part of you.
My grandpa's family didn't speak of it.
Their stories are buried with their dead.
Their skills sleep in the past.
They were told to be ashamed,
to hide from themselves.
But as Grandfather has told me
everything seeks balance.
Their blood now sings in my body.
It is awake and it teaches me.
As the sun walks backwards,
one of my relatives raised his bow
in anger and sadness.
His arrow flew and now here in the north,
I catch it.

Wait, Grandfather, these words,
where did they come from?
How are they on paper?
Did the trees write them or the sky?
Did the sea?

Lightening Man hit me on the head,
and words spilled out my fingers,
and look, now here they are on a page.
I wonder about this.

Grandfather sips his coffee,
gets up, throws another log on the wood stove.
Slowly the storm rolls by the cabin.
"Yes," says Grandfather,
"Sometimes that's the mystery for you."

Coyote comes in, shakes off the snow,
walks in four circles and curls up on the rug.
I look outside and breathing fog on a branch,
sits Eagle,
chirping.